I AM
CALM

How To Leave Your Worries Behind

Maria Robins

I AM CALM

How To Leave Your Worries Behind

Copyright © 2018 by Maria Robins
Animal Illustrations by Manqing Jin.

978-0-473-43848-7

The information contained in this book is intended to be educational and not for diagnosis, prescription or treatment of any health disorder whatsoever. The intent of the author is to offer information of a general nature to help you in your quest for emotional and spiritual wellbeing. In the event you use any of the information contained in this book for yourself, which is your constitutional right, the author and the publisher assume no responsibility for your actions.

Requests for publication should be addressed to:

Altreya Publishing Ltd
PO Box 90 256
Victoria Street West
Auckland, New Zealand 1142

A catalogue record for this book is available from the National Library of New Zealand.

INTRODUCTION

It's a busy world we live in these days and it's easy for things to get on top of us and leave us feeling overwhelmed. Some of us find it harder than others to stay calm when things happen that trigger our worries and fears, especially the young and the more sensitive.

This book is written in a simple and easy rhyming format for children who might be feeling anxious or worried, along with illustrations that reinforce the words in the story. It's designed to help provide coping tools that kids can use on a regular daily basis to keep their worries at bay but I hope that even the most stressed of adults will be able to relate to and apply the simple messages contained within!

May life become calmer and more relaxed for us all.

Keep Calm

All is Well

What we are here to learn today

Is how to stop worries from getting away

With letting us lead our happiest lives

By making us feel all anxious inside

We're going to find out how we can stop that

So we can relax, like a big happy cat

Think of your mind like a balloon filled with thoughts

Happy, excited and all other sorts

The same way that 1+1 = 2

Our thoughts join together, it's just what they do

Whatever we're thinking about will expand

And if we're not mindful, can get out of hand

Whoops, off it goes, we were fine just before

But the worry balloon is now starting to soar!

'Oh No!' we think, 'This is not going well'

'These thoughts I am thinking are

starting to swell'

Like a big worry-ball that starts to unravel

It's hard to believe just how far it can travel

We start to go round and around in a flurry

Adding in more thoughts to make us worry

We know that it's not a good thing to do

But most of us do it, oh yes it's true!

Not only kids but grown ups too

So we must train our minds to think something new

Here's a good way to turn this around

So that back in a CALM space your mind can be found

When you catch yourself thinking, 'It's no good, I'm stressed'

PAUSE... and instead think of how much you are blessed

The trick is to stop that thought right at the start

Before it can worm its way into your heart

As soon as that worry thought enters your mind

Try out this great trick to leave it behind

Pause and remember your Gratitude Cup

Don't let that negative thought trip you up!

Start thinking about the things you are glad of

Take your mind off the worry and onto the love

Maybe it's thinking of family or friends

Or a favourite thing again and again

Don't focus on the things of concern

Do not even give those thoughts a turn

Think of something nice that you like

Like eating an ice-cream or riding your bike

Say:

I AM CALM

I AM OK

I'm not getting sucked down with these
thoughts today

Instead I am rising above and beyond

Back to the HAPPY place where I belong

Here's another trick to get back on track

And push any negative thinking back

It's all about breathing, there's no need to hurry

This is a great way to get rid of the worry

You can do breaths out loud, you can do them inside

Doing deep breaths is like turning the tide

When you start to get anxious. just pause and delete

Think about nice things

Think of things that are neat

Take 3 long, slow breaths...

Breathe IN and breathe OUT

Right down to your belly, leaving no doubt

That as you breathe out, your worries will leave

And CALM now takes over, just slowly breathe

Think about good things, 1, 2 and 3

Deep breaths will help keep your mind worry-free

Keep breathing slowly, think of nice, happy stuff

And that worry-thought ball will be gone in a puff!

Say: NO! That thought does not belong here

This is only a 'trick thought' to give me a scare

I AM STOPPING that thought I don't want right this minute

I refuse to allow my mind to go in it

I AM moving my mind right now from what's wrong

Like changing the tune when I don't like a song

I know **I AM CALM**

I know **I'm OK**

I'm not getting sucked down with these thoughts today

Instead I AM thinking of something I like

A good feeling thought, a thought that is nice

At the same time I do this, I keep slowly breathing

And lo and behold those bad thoughts are leaving

I pause, take 3 breaths, think of nice things instead

To keep my mind calm and to clear out my head

Oh what a difference it makes when I do

I'm no longer stuck in the mind-worry stew

I AM only giving good thoughts a place

So that I can go back to my HAPPINESS SPACE

And when I stay in this space **I AM CALM**

Because now my thoughts can do me no harm

So remember...

When that worry-thought ball starts to unwind

Grab it and pull it right back into line

Catch it and stop it as soon as it starts

Bring your attention back into your HEART

Say:

I AM CALM

I AM OK

I'm not getting sucked down with these thoughts today

Take nice, slow, deep breaths... 1, 2, and 3

Breathing is very important you see

Let go of the fear, see it leaving your mind

So back in the HAPPINESS SPACE you can find

Keep thinking about a thing that you like

Imagine it, feel it and make yourself smile

It doesn't matter what that thing is

The trick is to focus on good, that's the biz

Pause, take 3 breaths, think of nice things instead

To keep your mind calm and to clear out your head

It might take some practice but practice makes
perfect

And the results I can promise are very well
worth it

The more you can do this, the more you will find

That instead of the worry ball...**YOU** will

UNWIND.

To receive updates on new I AM releases please email
altreyapublishing@gmail.com

If you found this book helpful, please leave a rating on
Amazon to help spread the word – thank you!

www.iamjournals.com

www.facebook.com/iamjournals

About the Author

Maria Robins was born in the Scottish heritage town of Dunedin, New Zealand and currently lives in Auckland, NZ. She loves words and writing and books, along with long walks at sunset and all things animal and nature.

Her goal is to inspire as many people as possible to believe in the power of having a positive mindset and grateful attitude so that they can enjoy their most joyful and meaningful lives.

Other I AM Books

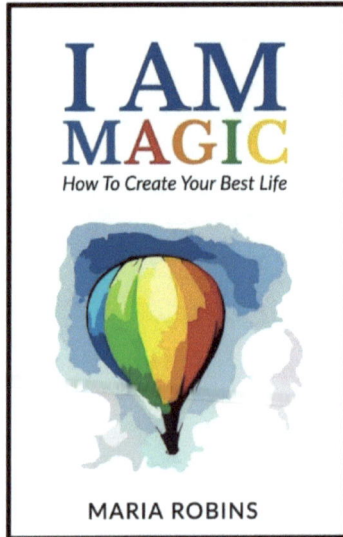

For children of all ages, especially the grown up ones!

Did you know that you think over 50,000 thoughts a day? Would you like to learn how to make those thoughts work *for* you instead of against you? No matter how old you are, learn how a simple two word statement can change your life in astonishing ways. You no longer have to leave your life to chance. I AM Magic shows you exactly how to take control of your own happiness and success.

Other I AM Books

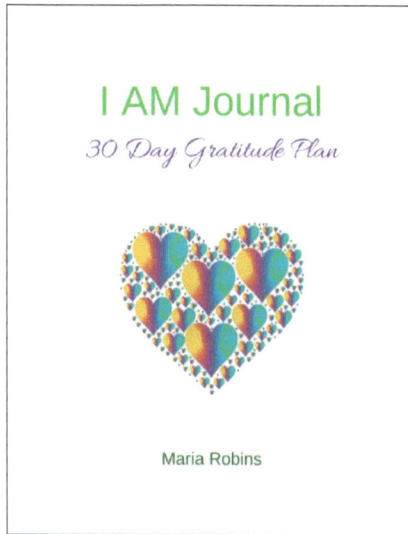

I AM Journal

30 Day Gratitude Plan

Maria Robins

Finding appreciation is one of the nicest things you can do for yourself and for those around you. Not only is it good to focus on the things in life that you are grateful for but it has the added bonus of attracting more good things into your life.

The first in the I AM Journals series, the 30 Day Gratitude Plan is designed to help you focus on the positive aspects in your life by writing them down each day and reviewing them on a weekly basis.

Notes:

Write down the things to do when you start to feel nervous or worried.
Here's a clue.....1, 2, 3.....

_____

_____

_____

_____

_____

_____

_____

_____

_____

_____

Notes:

Write down some happy things you can think about if you start to feel nervous or worried...

_____

_____

_____

_____

_____

_____

_____

_____

_____

_____